*The Essential Guide to
Presentation Software*

The Essential Guide to Presentation Software

Allison J. Ainsworth

Gainesville State College

Rob Patterson

McIntire School of Commerce,
University of Virginia

BEDFORD / ST. MARTIN'S

Boston ♦ New York

Manufactured in the United States of America.

4 3 2 1 0 9
f e d c b a

For information, write: Bedford/St. Martin's, 75 Arlington Street, Boston, MA 02116 (617-399-4000)

ISBN-10: 0-312-53819-7
ISBN-13: 978-0-312-53819-4

Acknowledgment

"The Plague of Powerpoint." Excerpt from *High Tech Heretic* by Clifford Stoll. Copyright © 1999 by Clifford Stoll. Used by permission of Doubleday, a division of Random House, Inc. and Brockman, Inc. on behalf of the author.

# PREFACE

The Essential Guide to Presentation Software is a versatile supplement for students who need a concise and affordable introduction to using presentation software. It has been designed to help public speakers understand the role that presentation aids can play in supporting speeches and to give students the training they need in planning and executing effective slide shows using Microsoft PowerPoint 2007. From developing audience-centered presentation aids and designing clean, visually appealing slide shows, to delivering dynamic speeches smoothly no matter the speech forum, this guide gives students the tools they need to build presentation aids that reinforce their speech goals and truly connect with their audiences. This guide can be used as a supplement in a wide variety of communication courses—especially introductory public speaking and human communication courses—and will be a valuable resource for speakers at every level, from those who have never created presentation aids to those who may simply require a brief refresher on the techniques for utilizing recent versions of PowerPoint.

The Essential Guide to Presentation Software uses a straightforward, cumulative approach to help students understand the functions of visual aids, and to prepare them to be adaptive speakers capable of giving confident, well-planned presentations. Over 50 illustrations from professional and student presentation aids visually demonstrate key concepts while helpful checklists, thought-provoking activities, and real-life examples highlight important points throughout. Topic coverage includes:

- An overview of the use, functions, pros, and cons of presentation software (Chapter 1)

- Advice on tailoring visual aids to best fit the audience and the speaking situation (Chapter 1)

- A discussion of different types of presentation aids and the ways that they can be used to best reach audiences (Chapter 2)

- Basic design principles for creating clear and pleasing slide shows (Chapter 3)

- A comprehensive walk-through of the important features of PowerPoint 2007 (Chapter 3)

- Tips on preparing presentation aids and guidelines for incorporating them into presentation delivery (Chapter 4)

v

- Best practices for presenting with PowerPoint slide shows, including advice on avoiding common pitfalls and technical glitches (Chapter 4)

This booklet is available either as a stand-alone text or packaged with *A Speaker's Guidebook, A Pocket Guide to Public Speaking, Speak Up: An Illustrated Guide to Public Speaking*, and a number of other Bedford/St. Martin's communication titles—including the booklets *The Essential Guide to Group Communication, The Essential Guide to Interpersonal Communication, The Essential Guide to Rhetoric*, and *The Essential Guide to Intercultural Communication*. For more information on these or other Bedford/St. Martins communication texts, please visit www.bedfordstmartins.com.

The approach and content of this text are based on the extensive teaching experience of Allison Ainsworth and owe much to Rob Patterson's original guide, *Using Presentation Software in Public Speaking*. Allison wishes to thank Jason Bewley, Dwight Lanier, and Chris Semerjian of the Institute of Environmental Spatial Analysis at Gainesville State College for their assistance with the GIS maps, the members of Sigma Chi Eta, the National Communication Association student honorary, who shared their experiences as student presenters on their local campuses and at conferences, and the communication professionals who contributed examples from personal and student works. She expresses much gratitude to her husband, Stuart, her daughters, Isabel and Grace, and her parents, Kim and Terri Powell. This book is indebted to the editorial contributions of Erika Gutierrez, Lai Moy, Ben Platt, Andrew Inchiosa, and Mae Klinger, and to an outstanding production team: Emily Berleth and Sarah Ulicny, all at Bedford/St. Martin's, and to the consummate professionals at Publishers Solutions.

CONTENTS

The Essential Guide to
Presentation Software

Introduction to Using 1
Presentation Software

In recent years, advances in presentation aid technology, such as new developments in presentation software and projection methods, have changed the requirements for public speakers, as well as enabled them to better connect with their audiences. In this digital age of online research, Web news sources, social networking, and blogging, many audience members have shorter attention spans and may prefer pictures, colors, and graphics to a straight speech without visual aids. As people rely more and more on visual cues rather than on printed text, it is not surprising that there is an increasing emphasis on the importance of presentation aids, and especially on using presentation software in speech making. Presentation technology is developing so quickly that communication research has difficulty keeping up with it. By the time you read this, you may be using a new type of software or technology that is not mentioned here. But not to worry! The topics covered in this guide will help you build a foundation for using presentation aids and software that you can apply to any new technologies that may come along.

The purpose of this guide is to assist you in making good choices when using presentation software in public speaking situations. Although the primary emphasis should always be on the oral rather than on the visual aspects of your speech, a basic knowledge of the mechanics of presentation software in general and Microsoft PowerPoint in particular is necessary and can be very valuable to you as a public speaker. While Adobe Persuasion, Apple Keynote, Gold Disk Astound, and other presentation software packages are also available, PowerPoint remains the most widely used. In fact, this is probably not the first time you have been asked to develop a PowerPoint slide show, or "stack," as some people call it. This guide will help you design an effective slide show as well as acquaint you with the 2007 version of PowerPoint, especially the new features that may be unfamiliar to you. (Additional support may also be found in the instructions that accompany your PowerPoint software package.) Throughout this guide, you will find copies of actual slides and images from both student presentations and the business world. These examples represent both effective and ineffective slides so you can see what and what not to do.

SPEECH FIRST, PRESENTATION AIDS SECOND

Presentation aids should be designed to increase the effectiveness of your speech. Think of presentation aids—computerized or not—as complements to, and

CHECKLIST

Steps in Preparing Speeches with Presentation Aids

1. Choose a topic.
2. Analyze your audience.
3. Choose your speech purpose, and create a thesis statement.
4. Conduct research, then write and revise the speech outline.
5. Plan and produce your presentation aids.
6. Practice your delivery.
7. Tweak your outline and presentation aids as needed.
8. Develop a contingency plan for the presentation.
9. Scout out the speaking site.
10. Set up the equipment and do a dry run.
11. Relax and give your presentation!

extensions of, your oral message. Presentation aids should never detract from or compete with your message.

Your speech outline should come before the presentation aid. Designing the PowerPoint slide show before writing your speech is like putting the cart before the horse. You will have a difficult time delivering the speech effectively and also knowing when to show the slides. Most of your preparation time for any speech should be spent researching, organizing, and outlining what you are going to say, not what you are going to show.

EFFECTIVE PRESENTATION AIDS ARE AUDIENCE CENTERED

Presentation aids can augment and support presentations and help the audience reach a higher level of understanding than they would by just listening to a speech. Presentation aids can help listeners process and retain information, capture their attention, and promote their interest in the speech, and can convey complex information concisely. Researchers Douglas Vogel, Gary Dickson, and John Lehman (1986)[1] found that individuals who heard a speech accompanied by presentation aids were more likely to perceive the speaker favorably; be persuaded; and attend to, comprehend, and agree with the speaker's basic thesis. To fully reap the benefits of using presentation aids, every presentation aid you create should be designed with your audience in mind. Effective com-

---

[1] Douglas R. Vogel, Gary W. Dickson, and John A. Lehman, *Persuasion and the Role of Visual Presentation Support: The UM/3M Study* (Minneapolis: University of Minnesota/3M, 1986).

municators address their listeners clearly and sincerely on a topic relevant to both the audience and the occasion. Developing slide content and design with your audience in mind will facilitate listener comprehension and retention of your message and will help you connect with your audience.

A BRIEF OVERVIEW OF AUDIENCE ANALYSIS

All good speakers analyze their audience, taking into account the audience's age, gender, ethnicity, and other demographic characteristics and their knowledge of the speech topic, as well as the speech setting. Be sure to think through all possible scenarios in order to accommodate most, if not all, of your audience. For example, when designing PowerPoint slides, remember that some audience members may be color blind. (See Chapter 3 for more information about design concepts and effective use of color in your PowerPoint slides and other visual aids.) How can you accommodate audience members who are visually impaired in more severe ways? One possible solution might be to include an audio component so they can "hear," even if they cannot fully see, the slide.

To ensure that your audience can reap the benefits of your aids, work to find out as much as possible about the speech forum before your presentation. Confirm that your presentation aids will fit the size and technological capabilities of your setting and the attributes of the audience so they can successfully reach your audience. For example, a large presentation space with a stationary audience of hundreds calls for one strategy, while a small poster session attended by a mobile audience that strolls around the space calls for another. The speaker in the large space should speak through a microphone and may want to project images onto a screen. On the other hand, the speaker at the small poster session would not benefit from designing an elaborate PowerPoint presentation but instead could prepare a poster that mobile audience members could view up close.

As well as investigating the speech setting, try to find out as much as you can about your audience before preparing your speech and presentation aids. This analysis may take the form of surveys or interviews that you design to reveal the demographic characteristics of your audience, what they already know about your speech topic, and how they may feel about the topic. Often, speakers are only able to administer surveys or interviews to a few members of a larger audience. If this is the case, make sure to choose a representative sample of the audience to get the most accurate information about your listeners. If you are unable to investigate audience members using questionnaires or interviews, then you can learn about the audience from other sources. Speaking at a conference? Check out the conference program for a sense of the attendees' areas of expertise and interest. Presenting to a community board? Members of the board may have short profiles online. A little research can yield very useful information. Finally, you should always consider and observe your audience. Ask yourself why they are attending your presentation, what they might already know about your topic, and how you can make your presentation to them most clear, interesting, and persuasive. Then ask yourself how you can design speech and presentation aids that are captivating, informative, and perhaps even entertaining *for this audience*. Next you will find a brief discussion of three common types of public speaking audiences: college students, professional listeners, and community members, which may help you begin your analysis on the right foot.

SPEAKING TO THE COLLEGE AUDIENCE

If you are currently taking a public speaking course, then making a speech to your classmates may be the only time you will ever be particularly familiar with your audience. To help you get acquainted, your instructor may have asked you to engage in an interactive exercise or may have had each student make a speech of introduction. Perhaps the student body as a whole shares a common background. Whether you attend a historically black college or university, a women's school, a community college in a small southeastern town with little diversity, or a college in a predominantly bilingual border community, you will probably be relatively familiar with the living conditions and income level of your classroom audience. And unless you have a large, nontraditional student population on your campus, most audience members will range from ages eighteen to twenty-four. Use this knowledge to your advantage, and tailor your aids to appeal to the audience as much as possible.

SPEAKING TO THE PROFESSIONAL AUDIENCE

Professional speaking situations may call for a different type of analysis. Though it is possible that you will present to colleagues with whom you are very familiar, it is also possible that you will need to make a presentation to a professional audience about whom you know very little, thus considering, observing, and researching your audience will be vitally important. It is also imperative that you understand the speech forum and prepare your aids to match that forum. When Greg was invited to speak at a health care business seminar, he did not know much about the age, gender, or ethnicity of his audience until he actually presented his speech to them. He did, however, learn other pertinent details about his audience by reviewing the program for the seminar. For instance, he knew that most audience members would be middle managers trying to generate more revenue for their health care businesses. He also knew that most would be knowledgeable about their field, but not experts in the specific topic area. Audience members had paid a fee to attend the conference and had chosen to attend his presentation, so Greg assumed that for these reasons most people would take notes. He then confirmed that the speech forum would allow for a slide show, so Greg decided to take plenty of time to make his presentation and to primarily use text-based slides. After you learn more about slide layout and design later in this guide, you should be able to come up with some other things Greg could have considered in analyzing his audience.

SPEAKING IN YOUR COMMUNITY

Speaking in your community can mean speaking to an extremely diverse audience with vastly different demographic characteristics. Whether you are stepping up at a town hall meeting or making a presentation at a community organization such as a club, an athletic league, or a religious or political group, make sure to find out as much as possible about your audience and prepare your aids and speeches to appeal to a variety of audience members. When presenting to a local volunteer group about the opportunity to help at the soup kitchen sponsored by her church, Mandy made sure that her speech and visual aids would appeal to both younger and older listeners. Furthermore, she took special care to present the topic so that even those not associated with her church or religion would feel welcome participating. Being a leader in the community means ensuring that your passions and messages translate clearly to *all* audience members.

PROS AND CONS OF USING PRESENTATION AIDS

In general, people like to look at images and objects more than they do words. The three-dimensional pop-up picture books you read as a child and the colorful, glossy, oversized coffee-table books many of us own as adults are good examples of our preference for the visual. In fact, many people are visual learners; that is, they learn best using visual materials, such as colorful images, maps, and photos. The primacy of the visual means that presentation aids have many benefits, but these benefits are balanced by certain risks. Understanding the potential benefits and drawbacks of presentation aids can help you as you move forward in developing aids to accompany your presentation.

Used effectively, presentation aids can

- help make complex ideas clear;
- create and maintain the audience's interest;
- help audience members retain what they are being told; and
- provide visual frameworks for presentations.

However, if not used effectively, presentation aids can

- distract the audience from the purpose of the speech;
- interfere with the smoothness of the speaker's presentation and, in the case of presentation software;
- cause unexpected technical glitches.

For more information about maximizing the opportunities afforded by presentation software and avoiding potential pitfalls, please see Chapter 4.

ACTIVITY

Evaluating Visual Aids

Think back to the last time you were in the audience when someone gave a speech using presentation software. In the chart that follows, list what you liked and disliked about the speaker's slide show. As you learn more about using presentation software appropriately, you will be able to think of ways this presentation could have been improved.

_____

_____

_____

_____

_____

PROS	CONS
_____	_____
_____	_____
_____	_____
_____	_____
_____	_____

Visual Aids Consisted of

_____

_____

_____

_____

_____

PROS	CONS
_____	_____
_____	_____
_____	_____
_____	_____
_____	_____

Presentation Software and 2
Other Types of Visual Aids

Presentation aids are simply artifacts that help speakers support their oral message, most often visually. Prior to the advent of presentation software, speakers depended on presentation aids such as posters, objects and models, charts and graphs, photographs, and maps. New presentation technology offers us unusual flexibility in the way we show visual aids to our audiences: it allows speakers to easily incorporate into one slide show diverse aids such as photos, text, maps, media clips, and interactive features. It is almost as if presentation software allows us to reflect the online environment with which we have become so familiar, where different forms of multimedia are always at our fingertips.

However, it remains useful to understand all individual types of presentation aids, not only because we can often incorporate into a slide show the attributes of nondigital aids to great effect but also because it is crucial for speakers to know which type of aid to use when. As a speaker, you have many options from which to choose, depending on the occasion, the setting, and the technology at your disposal, and a slide show may not always be the best choice. Speakers should always consider the speech forum and the audience's needs when choosing a particular aid. This chapter discusses the types of presentation aids you might consider. Even if you know that your presentation requires you to use PowerPoint, being familiar with the ways other visual aids function can help you think critically about your slide show and how it can better connect with the audience and support your message.

POSTERS

It may be appropriate in certain speaking situations to use a poster or tri-fold presentation board as your visual aid. Many professional conferences offer poster sessions where attendees can view in a large room posters and presentation boards displayed on tables. In these cases, posters are meant to be viewed from one to three feet away. Much of the advice about the appearance of PowerPoint slides also applies to the layout and design of a poster. You should always plan the layout of your poster or tri-fold presentation board several days before your poster session or presentation.

While posters *can* be used successfully in a larger speech setting, those designed for public speaking situations should be readable from twenty to thirty feet away, so speakers often struggle to effectively size fonts, graphics,

Alejandro, Meghan, David, and Philip pose with the poster they used for their presentation on inappropriate cell phone usage in college classrooms at the Southern States Communication Association Undergraduate Honors Conference in Louisville, Kentucky, April 2006.

ACTIVITY

Tri-Fold Presentation Board Design

Using the following diagram as a template, design your own tri-fold presentation board, labeling all of the elements that will compose the presentation aid for your speech.

Write a brief paragraph analyzing the speech setting for your upcoming speech, explaining whether and why, considering what you now know about presentation aids, a poster would be the correct aid to use.

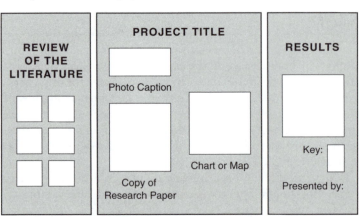

and photos. If the equipment is available at the forum, then presentation software used with a computer projector is often a better choice for presenting in larger speech sites. With presentation software, slides can be projected at a readable size, and the speaker can easily show, one after another, large charts or images.

OBJECTS AND MODELS

You probably used three-dimensional presentation aids when you were very young. Maybe you can remember bringing your favorite doll or book to your kindergarten show-and-tell day; or using the seashells you brought back from a beach trip over your second grade spring break to talk about what you did while you were on vacation; or building a model of the solar system or a volcano for your fourth grade science project.

In a presentation on how to set a table for a five-course meal, you might use a display table to show the various dishes, utensils, linens, and glassware that would be used during the meal, or you might use a tire from a NASCAR race car to talk about a pit crew's pre-race preparation process. You can also use objects to visually represent a statistical analysis. For example, to demonstrate the quantity of different trash and recycling receptacles in your building, you could bring in several clear cups and put different amounts of candies in each one to point out that it is more convenient to use trash cans rather than recycling bins.

This photo of ordinary clothespins is used as a presentation aid for a speech on little-known facts about a well-known object.
SOURCE: www.istockphoto.com

From left to right, these glasses contain 122, 52, 12, and 6 candies, respectively, representing the number of trash cans and paper, plastic, and glass recycling bins found in an office building.

Using candy this way is a good example of being creative when designing your presentation aid. However, make sure that any objects you choose fit the situation, are visible to your entire audience, and do not disturb the flow of your speech. It is a good idea to get approval from your speech instructor or the sponsor of your presentation before bringing in an atypical object to use as a presentation aid. A student giving a presentation on the different types of nonpoisonous snakes received approval to bring in a live snake as a prop. How-

REAL SPEAKERS IN ACTION

Less Is More

A glass artist making a presentation about handblown glass brought in nearly 100 pieces of her glass art, from paperweights to vases, as presentation aids. The audience was overwhelmed by so many examples. One or two glass pieces would have had a greater impact and would have allowed the artist to explain those pieces in greater detail, which would have been more interesting to the audience.

ever, other students in the class who had a snake phobia were given permission to leave the room during the student's presentation, disrupting the flow of his speech. For obvious reasons, weapons, alcohol, tobacco products, and drug paraphernalia are likely to be off-limits speech props.

Sometimes speakers want to bring in food to pass out to their audience. Always ask prior to bringing in food for your presentation whether any audience members have food allergies. You may also need to obtain permission to bring in food prepared in a home kitchen to serve your audience. Always think carefully about the type and quantity of props you will show and the manner in which you will show them.

Models, or scaled representations of objects, come in handy as presentation aids when it is not possible or practical to bring in the object itself. You might use a model if the object you are discussing is too large, such as James Madison's home, Montpelier; too small, such as a DNA molecule; or does not exist in today's world, such as the extinct mastodon. Set designers, architects, and engineers often make scale models to represent building projects, but this takes a lot of time, patience, and expertise. Unless you enjoy, and are good at, making models as a hobby, or you are enrolled in a set design or 3-D modeling course, it is probably best not to spend an inordinate amount of time gluing together a model. Instead, focus on writing your speech and preparing a simpler presentation aid.

This scale model of the Tower of London is on display inside of the tower.
SOURCE: www.wikipedia.com

REAL SPEAKERS IN ACTION

People as Presentation Aids

Speakers sometimes use other people as presentation aids. A presentation on organ donation might be enhanced if the speaker were accompanied by a person who had undergone a kidney transplant. Having a volunteer to demonstrate different types of golf swings could also make a presentation more vivid. And having a dance partner would obviously enliven a presentation on ballroom dancing. A student giving an impromptu presentation on valuable "found" objects in the classroom made a split-second decision to use her instructor as her "presentation aid," much to the amusement of the other students in the class. However, using people or animals as props can be unpredictable. You definitely need to be prepared for the unexpected when you share with someone else control of your speech's outcome!

PICTORIAL PRESENTATION AIDS

Although the aids discussed earlier can certainly be an excellent component in a slide show, this section discusses two-dimensional pictorial presentation aids, such as charts, graphs, photos, and clip art, that lend themselves especially well to display through presentation software. The presentation aids that follow work particularly well as part of a PowerPoint presentation, and speakers can also use presentation software and other computer applications to actually create or generate many of the aids, such as charts, graphs, or clip art, discussed next.

CHARTS AND GRAPHS

Typically, charts and graphs appear in six formats: pie chart, flowchart, organizational chart, line graph, bar graph, and column chart. All of these formats represent statistical information, quantities, or relationships between at least two things. Sometimes you can find a chart for your topic on a Web site; if you do, be sure to cite on your slide the source of the chart to avoid plagiarism. Sometimes you have the data and need to produce your own chart. PowerPoint's preprogrammed tools provide an easy way for you to design a chart.

A *pie chart* shows a circle divided into several "slices." This format is useful for showing percentages.

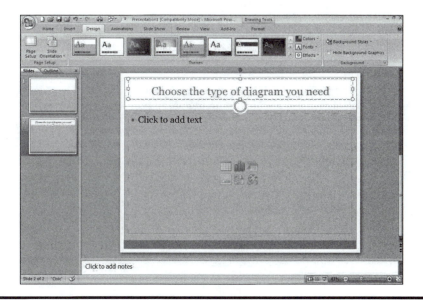

This screen shot from PowerPoint shows the instructions for selecting diagram tools.

SOURCE: Microsoft product screen shot reprinted with permission from Microsoft Corporation.

How useful do you find the college transcript in helping you evaluate job applicants' potential to succeed at your company?

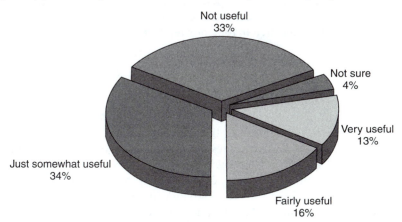

This pie chart was produced with PowerPoint.

SOURCE: Adapted from "Employers On Accountability Challenge," December 2007 by Peter D. Hart Research Associates for The Association of American Colleges and Universities.

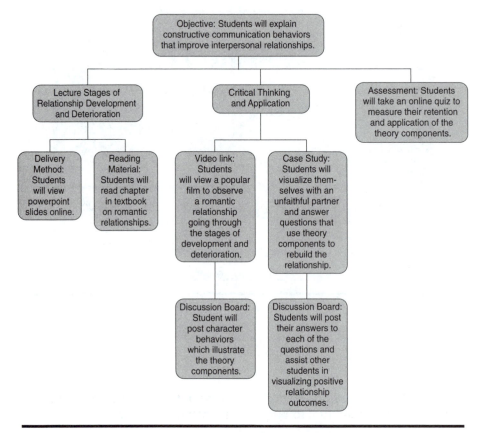

This flowchart demonstrates the process students go through when learning about constructive communication in romantic relationships.

A *flowchart* represents a process that evolves over time and across situations. The flowchart normally conveys steps, phases, or stages.

An *organizational chart* represents the structure of an organization, using boxes and lines to convey hierarchy, lines of authority, and other relationships.

The *line graph* is well suited to showing changes over time across two axes. It might show that the number of applicants accepted to James Madison University steadily increased from 1989 to 1999. By using more than one line with a unique color or pattern for each, you can show how things compare to each other over the same time period. For example, your graph could compare the number of applicants to James Madison University to the number of applicants to the University of Georgia.

Division of Land-Holdings

Mount Vernon Plantation

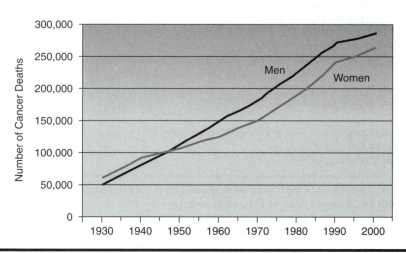

Mansion House Farm
Oversees All Operations
Primary Residence

| River Farm | Union Farm | Muddy Hole Farm | Dogue Run Farm |

This organizational chart demonstrates that Mansion House Farm was the core of the operation at George Washington's Mount Vernon plantation. The other farms below Mansion House Farm are positioned horizontally to each another, suggesting that they were equal, self-sustaining enterprises that produced for the whole.

Trends in the Number of Cancer Deaths Among Men and Women, US, 1930–2005

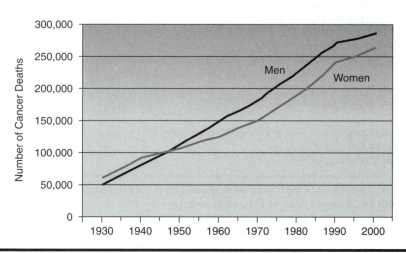

This line graph compares the number of cancer-related deaths of men and women over a seventy-five-year period.

SOURCE: U.S. Mortality Data, 2005, National Center for Health Statistics, Center for Disease Control and Prevention, 2008.

Bar graphs use horizontal bars to represent various values or quantities, while *column charts* use vertical bars to represent values or quantities. Either one can be used to represent the same values or quantities.

Tables represent data in rows and columns. An Excel spreadsheet is an example of a table. If in biology class you studied genetic traits such as eye color, then you may have recorded in a table dominant and recessive genes.

You should allow time in your presentation for audience members to read the details of the slide. Direct their attention to its important aspects, and explain the numbers or information being represented.

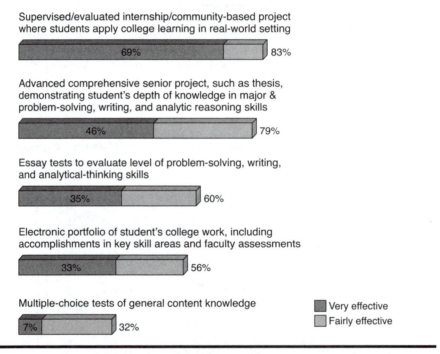

This bar graph explains employers' perceptions of the different assessments used to measure knowledge/skills of college graduates.

Source: Adapted from "Employers On Accountability Challenge," December 2007 by Peter D. Hart Research Associates for The Association of American Colleges and Universities.

Prevalence of Overweight and Obesity in the U.S.*

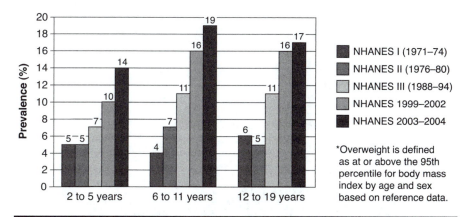

This column chart shows trends in obesity among different age groups of children.
SOURCE: National Health and Nutrition Examination Survey, 1971–1974, 1976–1980, 1988–1994, 1999–2002, National Center for Health Statistics, Center for Disease Control and Prevention, 2002, 2004, 2003–2004: Ogden CL, et al. "Prevalence of Overweight and Obesity in the United States, 1999–2004." *JAMA* 2006; 295 (13): 1549–55.

Employers Evaluate College Graduates' Preparedness in Key Areas

	Mean rating*	Very well prepared (8–10 ratings)*	Not well prepared (1–5 ratings)*
Teamwork	7.0	39%	17%
Ethical judgment	6.9	38%	19%
Intercultural skills	6.9	38%	19%
Social responsibility	6.7	35%	21%
Quantitative reasoning	6.7	32%	23%
Oral communication	6.6	30%	23%
Self-knowledge	6.5	28%	26%
Adaptability	6.3	24%	30%
Critical thinking	6.3	22%	31%
Writing	6.1	26%	37%
Self-direction	5.9	23%	42%
Global knowledge	5.7	18%	46%

* ratings on 10-point scale: 10 = recent college graduates are extremely well prepared on each quality to succeed in entry level positions or be promoted/advance within the company

This table used in a PowerPoint slide show demonstrates employers' evaluations of college graduates' likely success based on skills attained in college.
SOURCE: Adapted from "Employers On Accountability Challenge," December 2007 by Peter D. Hart Research Associates for The Association of American Colleges and Universities.

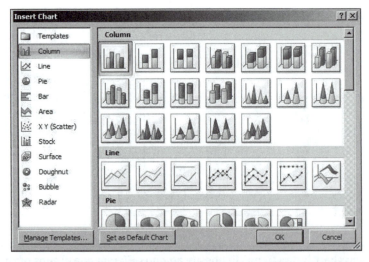

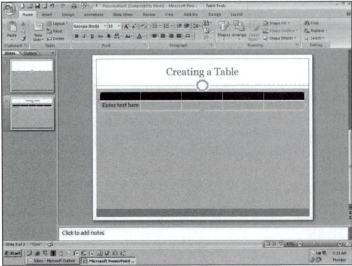

Both Microsoft Word and Microsoft PowerPoint include tools to help you create your own diagrams, charts, and tables.

SOURCE: Microsoft product screen shot reprinted with permission from Microsoft Corporation.

PHOTOGRAPHS, DRAWINGS, AND CLIP ART

A *photograph*, *drawing*, or other rendering can be a useful presentation aid when the actual object is unavailable. For example, a speech about the life and paintings of Vincent van Gogh would benefit from a photograph of his famous self-portrait, which you obviously cannot bring to your presentation.

You can also include photos that you have taken. Digital cameras make it easy to incorporate your own photos as a visual aid in your speech. For example, if you are giving a speech on different breeds of miniature dogs, then you could use your own photos of your own or your friend's miniature dog.

In our public speaking courses, we perform an experiment to demonstrate that photos projected onto a screen are more clearly visible than photos held up in front of an audience. First we hold up a 5 × 7 photo of an animal and ask the class to identify it. Next we project the same photo onto a screen and ask students to repeat the exercise. Every year, the students in the back of the room are unable to tell whether the animal in the 5 × 7 image is a dog or a horse, but when the same photo is projected, the species is obvious.

A presentation on clothespins might include information on the manufacture of clothespins in China, the use of iconic art for home display, and the use of simple household objects as modern art. The speaker might then bring up the fact that a forty-five-foot tall steel clothespin sculpture stands near City Hall in Philadelphia.

Photos or diagrams can also tell a story. A series of pictures can illuminate a process or show how something changes over time.

A self-portrait painted in oil on canvas by Vincent van Gogh, a Dutch Postimpressionist artist, in 1887.

SOURCE: www.wikipedia.com

When this photo was projected
onto a screen, it revealed a new-
born quarter horse standing
on wobbly legs, not a large dog.

The famous Philadelphia
Clothespin sculpture, 1976,
by Claes Oldenburg

SOURCE: www.worldofstock.com / © 2008 Daria
Mochan and World of Stock.

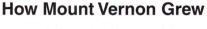

How Mount Vernon Grew

The house George Washington lived in as a boy,
and eventually rented from his brother.

Mount Vernon after the enlargement made during
1759 in preparation for Washington's marriage to Martha.

The 1759 house was extended during 1774 to the right, to supply
private living quarters. A similar wing to the left was begun in 1776.

In his presentation on Mount Vernon, Chris illustrated how Washington added on to the original house over time by showing this series of drawings.

A photograph's or drawing's value as a visual aid stems from the way in which it is presented. Passing individual photographs around the room is not effective, since audience members view them at different times (many of them after you have moved on to the next point in your presentation). When a projection system is not available, the best way to show a photo or drawing is to enlarge it as much as possible on a copier. (Commercial copy shops do this all the time.) If there is an old-fashioned overhead projector in the room, then you could print your digital photo onto a transparency sheet and display it that way. (Transparency sheets are available at office supply stores and can be put in computer printers just like paper.)

Clip art images can be cartoons, animated drawings, images, or photos stored in your presentation software or downloaded from the Internet. Using clip art may be the best option if you cannot find a high-quality photo of the item, cannot obtain permission to use the photo, or want a generic representation or symbol of something.

Clip Art Examples of Students

These clip art representations depict in different ways students in a classroom.

The tone of your presentation should determine which type of images you use. Realistic photos may be more appropriate for speeches about serious issues, while cartoons may be more appropriate for lighthearted, entertaining topics.

MAPS

Maps work well for presenting the spatial layout of an area. They also can serve as effective symbols. A map of Route 66 in the 1950s could be used to evoke what that iconic highway has meant to American culture. Maps can help your audience see the geographical relationship among things.

Maps may also show processes or stages. For example, a map accompanying a speech about the U.S. Merchant Marine's role in World War II could show the paths of merchant ships in the Atlantic Ocean and Pacific Ocean and the dates merchant ships were lost at sea due to enemy fire.

Maps can also provide a geospatial analysis of a particular set of data.

During presidential elections, news networks use maps of the entire country to indicate how people voted (i.e., "blue" states and "red" states).

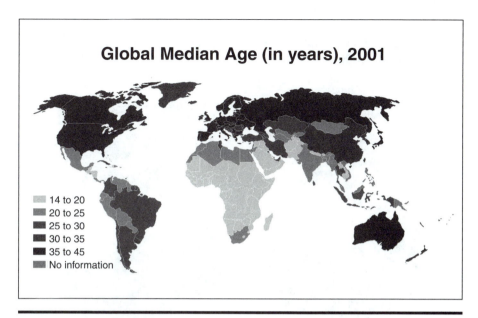

This map of the Global Median Age in Years shows the distribution of age ranges around the world, as of 2001.

SOURCE: www.wikipedia.com

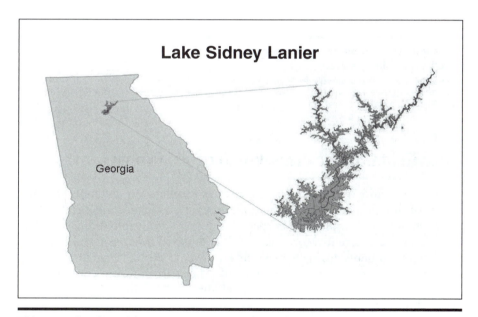

This map, developed for a presentation on land usage and conservation around Lake Lanier in Georgia, shows where the lake is located in the state.

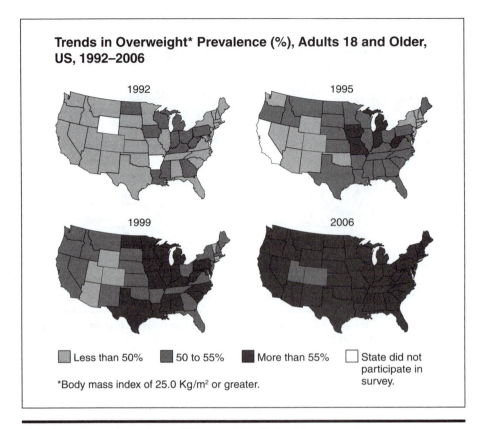

Trends in Overweight* Prevalence (%), Adults 18 and Older, US, 1992–2006

1992   1995

1999   2006

☐ Less than 50%   ■ 50 to 55%   ■ More than 55%   ☐ State did not participate in survey.

*Body mass index of 25.0 Kg/m² or greater.

This slide uses a single-layer GIS map of the United States to demonstrate one specific variable by state.

Source: Behavioral Risk Factor Surveillance System, CD-ROM (1984–1995, 1998) and Public Use Data Tape (2004, 2006), National Center for Chronic Disease Prevention and Health Promotion, Centers for Disease Control and Prevention, 1997, 2000, 2005, 2007.

MULTIMEDIA: MUSIC CLIPS, VIDEO CLIPS, AND WEB SITES

Music, video, and Web materials can serve as excellent presentation aids in a variety of situations. Speakers often utilize these types of aids independently of a slide show. For example, for her speech about old-time radio dramas, Andrea burned several different recordings to CD and played them using a boom box at the right moments during her speech. However, if she had wanted to also expose the audience to images and text, and if her speech forum contained the proper equipment, then a slide show, including audio clips, may have been a better choice.

The Internet and other multimedia sources have expanded the possibilities for information you can import into your PowerPoint slides. An audio clip of a song can be downloaded and added to your slide; a presentation on Elvis Presley and his different music genres takes on new meaning when the audience can hear twenty seconds of a song clip at the appropriate time during your speech. Video clips from YouTube and similar Web sites can also be imported into your speech. One successful student speaker imported a Dove soap commercial video clip into a PowerPoint slide show to help demonstrate the impact of media images of beauty on young girls. As with any presentation aid, however, you must not allow the audio or video clip to take control of your speech. You the speaker must remain the primary source of information and keep the audience's attention.

You can embed a Web site link directly into your PowerPoint slide to take your audience to a particular image or information source without interfering with the transition from one slide to the next. Of course, the presentation room must have Internet access in order for you to be able to include links to Web-based sources.

3 Designing and Creating Your Slide Show

Now that you have considered why you use a presentation aid, how to tailor a presentation aid to your audience, the pros and cons of such aids, and the basic functions of different types of presentation aids, you are ready to start developing your PowerPoint slide show. This chapter first presents design principles that can help you create your slides and then offers real techniques to help you implement these principles.

BASIC DESIGN PRINCIPLES

Simple, uncluttered slides work best, regardless of the detail or complexity of your speech. Keep borders plain, use colors wisely, and follow a consistent template throughout. As a rule, text slides should contain no more than six words per line and six lines per slide (the 6 × 6 rule). Each slide should flow to the next one in the same smooth way that each section of your speech transitions to the next.

You should aim for your PowerPoint show to look as professional as possible. Speakers are often judged by the clarity, accuracy, and usefulness of their presentation aids.

Different situations may call for different approaches. If you are going to be teaching young children, for instance, then you will want to consider how best to engage young minds as you design your presentation aids. Do not forget to consider your audience as you design your slide show! The following sections further explain basic design principles that will help you create a slide show your audience will follow and enjoy.

DECIDING ON THE RIGHT TYPE AND NUMBER OF SLIDES

We recommend that you look at your speech outline to get an idea of how many slides you will need to illustrate your speech. Some experts say you should use two to five slides for every seven minutes of speaking time. A twenty-minute speech, then, would incorporate six to fifteen slides. In your effort to limit the number of slides, avoid crowding too many photos or too much text onto one slide. Each slide should make a different point with your audience and be thought of as a stand-alone unit.

Claude Monet 1840–1926	Woman with Parasol, 1875

Impression, Sunrise 1872	Water Lilies, 1914–1917

Your knowledge of your topic is evidenced by the quality of the slides you use to support your ideas. A speech on the stages of Claude Monet's work was enhanced by the four slides showing different paintings from each of the stages, making each stage clear to the audience.

It is always best to have too few slides than too many. Ultimately, you are the best judge of how many slides are right for the presentation. As you decide on the number of slides to use, keep in mind that if "a picture is worth a thousand words" then images may make better slides than pure text. Fewer slides provide an increased opportunity for you to make eye contact with your audience. Often, an abundance of slides will increase a speaker's tendency to talk to the slides and not to the audience.

Using blank slides between text or image slides can enable your audience to better comprehend your ideas and see transitions from one idea to the next. This use of blank slides can also help the audience focus on you the speaker rather than on the text or image on your last slide. You can also use transition slides, which have one single, simple visual that ties in with your speech. A speaker giving a presentation on the Great Depression while impersonating Franklin D. Roosevelt used a slide with the Presidential Seal on it in between his other slides, which helped create a transition and enhanced the dramatic aspects of his presentation.

CHECKLIST

Using Your Outline to Plan Your Slides

1. Print out a copy of your speech outline.

2. Highlight the first line of each section that you feel needs a text- or image-based slide.

3. Open up your presentation software program, and start a new document.

4. Select your design, and then create one blank slide for each highlighted line of text on your outline.

5. Title each slide, and make sure to save the draft slide show under a descriptive title.

6. Use your outline and the draft document to decide on the text and/or images for each slide.

Finally, your presentation should always end with a complete source list from the "Works Cited" page of your paper or outline. It is not necessary to read the references to your audience at the end of your presentation, but do leave the reference slide up when answering audience members' questions.

UTILIZING COLOR AND CONTRAST TO YOUR ADVANTAGE

Color is a powerful, nonverbal tool that can enhance or detract from the effectiveness of your speech. The colors on your slides should have some relationship to the topic you are addressing. Soft colors such as pastel greens and blues have such a soothing effect that many medical offices and hospitals use them to help patients relax. Oranges, reds, and deep gold tend to get people excited. If your speech calls for your audience to empathize, then use cool colors such as pale blues, greens, or lilacs. Soft pink, which brings out skin tones, works well when you are showing facial images. If you are trying to motivate, inspire, demonstrate movement, or jolt your audience, then brighter and warmer colors should be used. Remember, cooler colors are better for creating a solemn tone, and warmer colors are better for capturing attention. Whites or neutrals generally make the best background color for your slides because of the high contrast they create between the text or image and the background. Light-colored fonts on a white, neutral, or pastel background or dark colors on a bright-red or dark background are ineffective, because the similar shades cause the text to blend into the background. Also keep in mind that color-blind persons cannot distinguish between some colors. To meet their needs, use black type on a white or neutral background, but if you are incorporating colors other than black and white, then make sure there is a high contrast between

Even though this sample slide is reproduced here in black and white, it demonstrates an inappropriate use of color (hot-pink sunset, orange background, yellow letters). Running similar colors side by side leaves little contrast between background and text and reduces readability.

adjacent colors, and differentiate slide elements with factors other than color, such as font size, underlining, and italics.

Normally you should use no more than two colors, in addition to the background color, on a single slide in order to prevent the slide from looking too busy. Some PowerPoint preprogrammed slide templates have more than three colors, but these multiple-color combinations are designed to be harmonious.

BEST PRACTICES FOR USING TEXT ON SLIDES

We have already covered the fact that text should contrast with background color to increase its visibility. Font type and size are also important considerations. Select an easy-to-read font such as Times New Roman, Arial, or Calibri. Minimum font size when the audience is twenty to thirty feet away from the screen is 24; when the audience is more than thirty feet away from the screen, the minimum size is 32. The audience should not have to squint to read your text.

The text on your slide should complement, not replace, your speech itself. If your audience can read along as you speak every word printed on the slide, then you have too much text on the slide. Also, audience members may become frustrated if you advance to the next slide before they have had time to read the current one. For some topics and slides, the 6 × 6 rule may not apply, since six words per line and six lines per slide would be too many. Your topic may only require titles or photo captions.

REAL SPEAKERS IN ACTION

An Audience Perspective — Middle School Open House

When the principal started her presentation at a sixth grade open house, she noticed that many audience members were leaning forward and squinting because the font size was too small. However, instead of stopping the slide show, the principal let it continue for the next forty minutes, with the audience unable to read a single word. The slide show was absolutely useless as a presentation aid, only serving to annoy the audience. The principal would have been better off apologizing for the illegible slides and shutting them off as she continued to speak, telling her audience that anyone who was interested could stop by the school office the next day to pick up a printout of the slides.

A five-to-ten minute speech will require less text than a longer presentation. The audience for Greg's hour-long speech about billing and workers' compensation revenue needed to absorb large amounts of information. Greg spent five minutes explaining the information presented on each text-based slide.

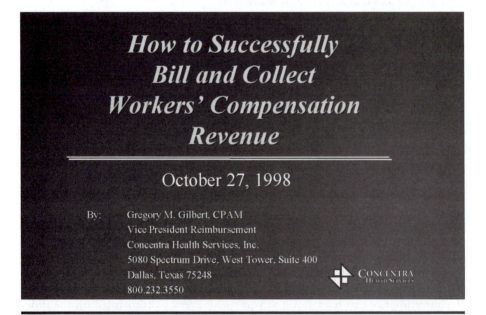

How to Successfully Bill and Collect Workers' Compensation Revenue

October 27, 1998

By: Gregory M. Gilbert, CPAM
Vice President Reimbursement
Concentra Health Services, Inc.
5080 Spectrum Drive, West Tower, Suite 400
Dallas, Texas 75248
800.232.3550

CONCENTRA
Health Services

Greg's cover slide from his presentation in San Diego. Greg's cover slide has no border and the font size is large, with plenty of blank space around it, making the slide easy to read quickly. As a general rule of thumb, your audience should spend at least 90 percent of the presentation listening and no more than 10 percent of the presentation reading.

CONSIDERING LAYOUT

The layout of your slide is also an important component of audience comprehension. The size and number of photos, charts, and maps, and their placement on the slide, will influence the effectiveness of your presentation aid. No more than one or two images per slide should be shown. Use a title or caption to label your photo.

This is an example of a slide with too many photos on it.

This slide is well proportioned in terms of the size of the photo, the size and weight of the text, and the amount of blank space surrounding the photo and text.

Your images should make a point, reinforce verbal descriptions, and support the overall goal of the speech. Note that high-resolution images require substantial disk space and may stall older computers; saving images in jpeg format will give you the highest-quality image with the smallest file size.

If you scan or download images from outside sources, then you must also consider copyright implications. Whenever content is copied from a document or a Web site, the source should be credited on the screen and in your oral presentation. Make sure to leave room for this in your layout.

> *"It was only when I was 22 years old and moved to New York, where people of different colors, beliefs, and sexual orientations are embraced, that I learned to appreciate my brown skin, wide nose, straight, black hair, and five-foot stature."*
>
> Tricia Capistrano (2006, June 19). Emil's Big Chance Leaves Me Uneasy. *Newsweek*, 26, 72–75.

This slide with a paraphrased quote cites the source using proper American Psychological Association (APA) style.

MAINTAINING FLUENCY AND CONSISTENCY IN YOUR SLIDE SHOW

Just as it is important for your speech to flow smoothly and logically, it is best for one slide to flow smoothly into the next. This means making sure that your slide content is organized in a way that makes sense in relation to your speech. Using your speech outline to develop your slide show can assist you in ensuring good organization of slide content. Maintaining fluency and consistency also requires general design elements, such as color, font and layout choices, to remain the same from one slide to another. Visual inconsistencies from slide to slide can be distracting to your audience, and you want to avoid them unless you have carefully chosen to utilize a design change, such as a new background color or font, to emphasize a specific image or phrase. Your slides should act as a visual and conceptual whole to help your audience understand the points

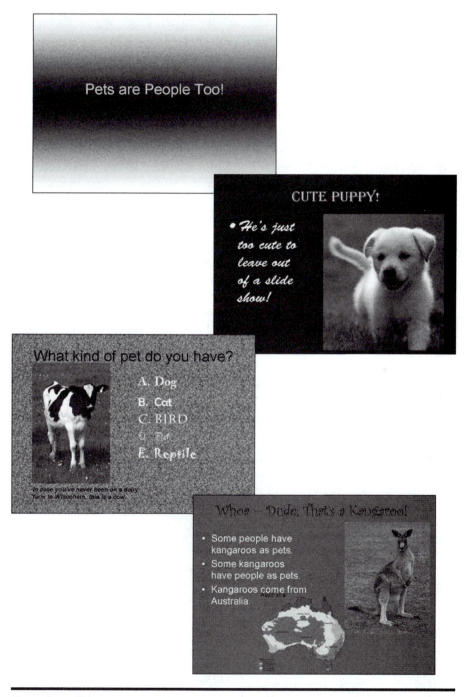

These four slides accompanying a presentation on pets are visually inconsistent and lack flow.

you are trying to make. If you are making a group presentation, then work together to ensure that each group member's section of the PowerPoint slide show is consistent with the other sections.

As a general rule, PowerPoint animation features should be avoided because they tend to disrupt visual flow and consistency and can prevent fluent delivery. Animation should be limited to slow and simple transitions of words or sentences in a list. Letters dropping or sliding in like a race car are distracting and annoying to most audience members. Additionally, you may find it difficult to change slides that contain animations when using some presentation equipment, so a particular slide may not match what you are saying.

APPLYING DESIGN PRINCIPLES USING MICROSOFT POWERPOINT 2007

Now that you have reviewed the basic design principles for creating slide shows, it is time to delve further into how you can implement these principles in PowerPoint 2007. PowerPoint offers a wealth of options, the sheer profusion of which can sometimes be confusing. This section introduces and explains the tools and techniques to which you will most often turn and discusses how you can utilize them most effectively.

FAMILIARIZING YOURSELF WITH TOOLBARS AND PRESENTATION OPTIONS

When you open PowerPoint 2007, you will see seven tabs at the top of the page: Home, Insert, Design, Animations, Slide Show, Review, and View. By clicking on any of these tabs, you can access a menu unique to the tab you choose.

The Home menu allows you create new slides and edit the fonts for existing slides.
SOURCE: Microsoft product screen shot reprinted with permission from Microsoft Corporation.

As you delve into this section, you will learn about many of the features of the other menus. Before you begin to work with PowerPoint, it can help to explore the options presented by the multiple tabs and menus to become familiar with what can be a complicated display.

In the previous section, we discussed some of the considerations regarding decisions about the right type and number of slides for your presentation.

PowerPoint offers three presentation modes: Slide Layout, Design Template, and Blank Presentation. Each will enable you to make a variety of design choices for your slides, and each has specific advantages and limitations. As you continue to read about these presentation modes, take into account the aesthetic principles that we examined earlier.

Slide Layout

Slide Layout enables you to choose from nine Office Themes that will provide the general structure for a slide. During your presentation, you will most likely want to vary the theme of the slides you create. The Office Themes included in Slide Layout have various purposes: for instance, a "Blank" or "Section Header" slide could act as a transitional slide and help your audience focus on your words instead of the content of the previous slides.

Design Template

Design Template expands significantly the number of available choices regarding the appearance of your slides. You can select from approximately twenty-one themes, all of which can be adjusted by modifying the color scheme, fonts, and effects. Once you choose a theme and revise its visual characteristics, Design Template will implement this theme as the consistent appearance for all of the slides in your presentation.

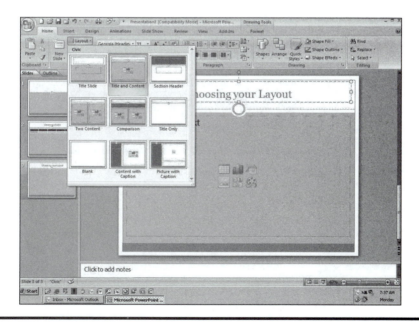

You can access the nine Office Themes from the Layout pull-down menu.

SOURCE: Microsoft product screen shot reprinted with permission from Microsoft Corporation.

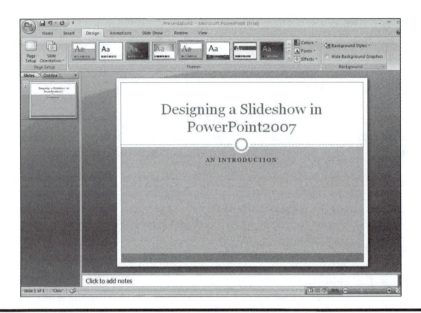

When choosing a theme in Design Template, consider how its appearance will support the content of your presentation.
Source: Microsoft product screen shot reprinted with permission from Microsoft Corporation.

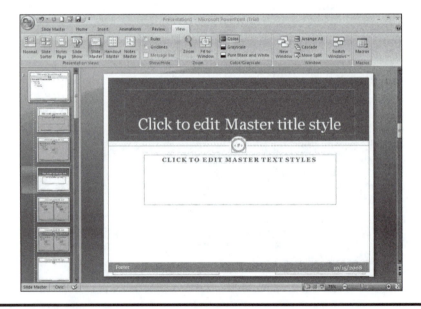

You can also access the Slide Master View from the View menu.
Source: Microsoft product screen shot reprinted with permission from Microsoft Corporation.

When you create a presentation that employs Design Template, Power-Point automatically introduces a Slide Master View with which you can control the text styles for a variety of different slide formats.

Blank Presentation

Among the three presentation modes, Blank Presentation is the most flexible, because you must choose every component of the slide's layout, color, font, and organization. The disadvantage of this mode is, in a sense, the same as its main advantage: you must design every element of each slide you include.

MAKING EFFECTIVE CHOICES ABOUT COLOR AND CONTRAST WITHIN THE PRESENTATION MODES

As you choose and then begin to work with one of these presentation modes, remember to always consider how the choices you make regarding color and contrast will complement your presentation. In Design Template, you encounter a wide sample of options as you determine the color scheme and fonts for your presentation. When working with Design Template, or when making choices of any kind that deal with color and contrast, remember the key points outlined in the previous section. First, the colors you use for your presentation should highlight your subject matter rather than clash with it. In addition, slides should always be clear and uncluttered so your audience can easily read them and comprehend their meaning. When you are developing your own color scheme in either the Slide Layout or Blank Presentation mode, you should avoid using more than two colors, excluding the background color.

A CLOSER LOOK AT TEXT OPTIONS

When you work in any of the presentation modes, a sample text box will appear in which you can enter the written content for the slide. (For some Office Themes and for many of the Design Template options, more than one sample text box will appear.) You can type and revise the text for the slide much as you would in a word processing program. At any point, you can change not only the content of your text but also its style. The numbering, bullet points, and dash symbols that automatically appear to organize your main and secondary ideas are default settings in some templates; you can disable these settings if you want to organize your text in a manner tailored to your particular speech.

LEARNING THE VIEWING OPTIONS FOR SLIDES AND PRESENTATIONS

In addition to learning the different options for formatting slides, you should familiarize yourself with the alternatives that PowerPoint 2007 offers for viewing the slides that comprise your presentation.

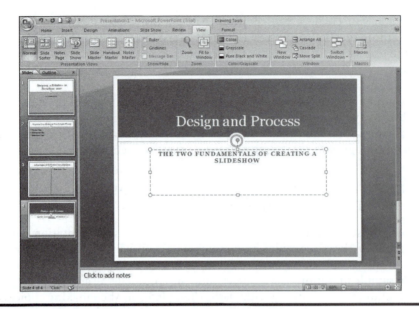

In most instances, the Normal View will be your default view.

SOURCE: Microsoft product screen shot reprinted with permission from Microsoft Corporation.

Normal View

This is the primary view you will use when creating and editing your slides. The slide on which you are currently working will appear at the center of the screen, with the other slides in the presentation visible to the left. At the bottom of the screen is a text box in which you can enter notes about a slide.

Slide Sorter View

Slide Sorter View allows you to look at all of the slides in your presentation at once. This view is particularly helpful to use as you think about how many slides to include, as well as whether your slides work well together aesthetically.

Notes Page View

This view emphasizes the notes section that also appears in the Normal View. If your preparation for your presentation is more dependent on notes, then you may find this view extremely helpful; otherwise, you may not have any need for it. The Notes Master View (accessible from the same toolbar from which you can access the Notes Page View) enables you to format the appearance of your note section in the same way the Slide Master View functions for slides.

Slide Show View
This view reflects how your presentation will appear when you project it. Similar to the Slide Sorter View, the Slide Show View allows you to view your presentation as a whole, an ideal way to examine the visual continuity of your slides.

VIEWING OPTIONS AND LAYOUT QUESTIONS

As mentioned earlier, the Normal View is the primary view you will use when creating and editing slides. Consequently, it is also the view in which you will be making most decisions about the layout of your slides. Remember to take into account not only the number of elements you include in a slide but also the proportions and arrangement of these elements. The Slide Show View offers another way to view the slides you have created and can be especially helpful in checking that the layout of a slide works effectively and is properly proportioned.

INCORPORATING VISUAL INSERTS INTO YOUR SLIDES

We discussed in previous sections how images, charts, and other inserts may support a speaker's goals and contribute to the successful layout of a slide. Here we review the options that PowerPoint provides for including and modifying a range of visual inserts.

Pictures
You can insert photos from your own personal files or draw relevant photos from online image sources. Corbis.com (pro.corbis.com) is a rich source for images, many of which you can download for a small cost. Google (www.google.com) and Yahoo! (www.yahoo.com) both have search tools that allow you to search exclusively for images. Shutterstock (www.shutterstock.com) and Photo License (www.photolicense.com) both allow you to purchase royalty-free photographs for use. Photo License, Jupiter Images (www.jupiterimages.com), and FreeFoto.com (www.freefoto.com) also offer free downloadable images. Should an image you download from the Internet or scan from another source include text that is not legible, use the image-cropping tool to remove the text from your slide; never include text on your slide that your audience cannot read. You may need to retype the photo caption in a larger font size on your slide. The best way to determine whether your text is too small is to view your slide on the projection screen in the room where you will be speaking. While some of the sample slides included in this guide may look too small as printed here, they are effective when projected during a presentation.

You can use the PowerPoint cropping tool to delete text that is too small.
Source: Microsoft product screen shot reprinted with permission from Microsoft Corporation.

Apart from using the image-cropping tool, there are additional ways to alter an image's appearance. Once you have inserted an image, you can use the Shape Outline tool, which you can find within the Home menu, to create an outline for that image to create greater contrast with the background color.

Clip Art

You can search for images in the PowerPoint Clip Art Gallery, the link to which is located on the Insert menu. Although the Clip Art Gallery is sizable, it is most helpful as a source for generic images.

Charts

The Chart tool, which is also accessible from the Insert menu, offers a variety of choices regarding the kind of chart you wish to include. Depending on the nature of the data you will be representing in the chart, you could insert a bar or line graph or a pie chart, among many choices.

After you choose the data format that best suits your purpose, you can insert the data with which you are working into the chart you have created.

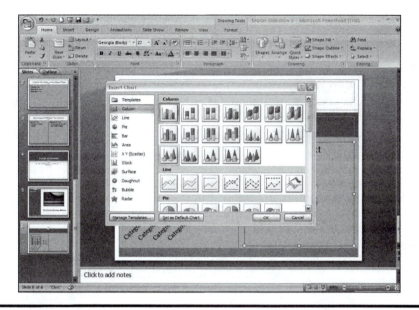

PowerPoint provides a range of options regarding the types and designs of charts you can insert.

Source: Microsoft product screen shot reprinted with permission from Microsoft Corporation.

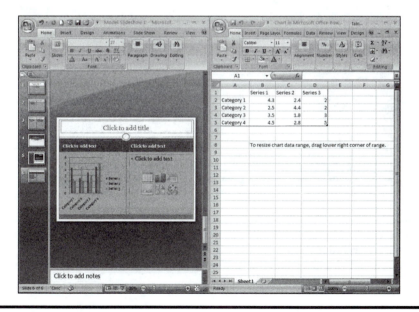

A spreadsheet will open automatically once you insert a chart, allowing you to input and modify your data.

Source: Microsoft product screen shot reprinted with permission from Microsoft Corporation.

Tables

The Insert menu also offers the option of creating a table. When you first insert a table, you will assign the number of rows and columns, but you can add or subtract rows and columns at any point.

You can adjust many aspects of a chart or a table once you have created one. When selecting a color scheme for either, remember to consider how the chart or table will appear against the background of the slide. Try to make the chart or table as legible as possible in order to best highlight the significance of the data it represents.

SmartArt Graphics

Another option you can choose from the Insert menu is the SmartArt icon. SmartArt Graphics can organize a more limited amount of information than charts and tables can, but they are especially helpful for depicting processes, cycles, hierarchies, and relationships.

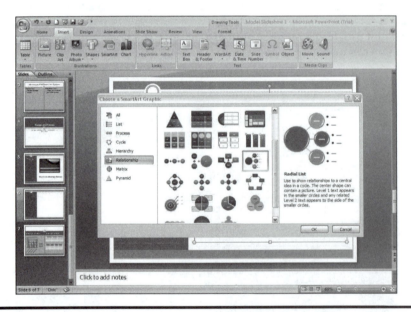

A Radial List, one SmartArt Graphic option, could be used to illustrate a sequence of connected relationships.

SOURCE: Microsoft product screen shot reprinted with permission from Microsoft Corporation.

INTRODUCING MULTIMEDIA CLIPS IN YOUR PRESENTATION

It is also possible to include audio, video, or Web content into your slide show. Because you want to avoid incorporating too many elements into your slide show, making it difficult to follow, consider first whether the multimedia clip you want to include is integral to your presentation.

Sound

You can choose an audio clip from either your computer's collection or from a compact disk and include it in a slide, using the Insert menu. Once you have inserted a sound clip, you can adjust when, how, and at what volume it will play during your slide show.

Movie

The Insert menu also enables you to insert a video clip by selecting the Movie icon. Once you select this icon, you can choose whether you want to insert a video clip from your own files by clicking on "Movie from File," or if you want to insert a video clip from the Clip Art Gallery by clicking on "Movie from Clip Organizer." The key difference between incorporating a video clip from your own files into a presentation and including any other visual or multimedia insert is that you will only be linking to this video clip from a slide; a video clip from your own collection will not be a permanent, embedded component of the slide. As a result, if your presentation incorporates such a video clip, then you must ensure that you save that clip in the same folder in which you saved your presentation. Because the steps you must take to successfully insert a video clip are slightly more involved than they are for other inserts, you may find it helpful to refer to Microsoft's PowerPoint Web site (www.office.microsoft.com/en-us/powerpoint/default.aspx) for more detailed instructions.

Web Content

Another way to include a video clip is to create a URL link that will connect you directly to a video available on the Web. Both Google Video (www.video.google.com) and Yahoo! Video Search (www.video.search.yahoo.com) function the same way the image-based search engines described earlier do, allowing you to search specifically for video clips. YouTube (www.youtube.com) offers a massive collection of video clips. CNN Video (www.cnn.com/video) contains a large collection of video clips especially relevant to current affairs.

You can also use this method to exhibit any other form of Web content; for instance, you could insert a link to a Web site as an introduction to a discussion of that Web site. There are several ways to link to a Web site from within a PowerPoint presentation. You can type the actual URL on the slide and, when you are making your presentation, click on the highlighted URL and go directly to the site. However, some URLs are too long or would be distracting to the flow of your speech. You can link any image, such as a corporate logo, to the actual URL by selecting the Hyperlink option on the Insert menu and by typing the URL in the prompt box. The URL will be hidden from the audience, but the link to the Web site will function smoothly. If you do choose to incorporate Web-based content, then you must ensure that your speech forum is wired for Internet access.

WORKING WITH TRANSITION EFFECTS AND TEXT ANIMATIONS

As noted in the previous section, many of the transition effects and text animations available in PowerPoint can quickly become disorienting and distracting to an audience. Because your slide show presentation is meant to augment your speech, you will most likely want to include only the least invasive transition effects and animations, if you decide to use them at all.

Transition Effects

When selecting the Animations menu, you will encounter a range of options for modifying the way in which one of your slides will flow into the next. You can select a sound that will accompany the transition between slides, as well as the speed at which this transition will occur.

Using the Animations menu, you can adjust whether slides will advance with a mouse click or after a set period of time has elapsed.

Source: Microsoft product screen shot reprinted with permission from Microsoft Corporation.

Text Animations

The Animations menu also allows you to develop custom animations for any element of a slide. Once you click on the Custom Animation icon and select the element you want to animate, you can modify how that element will enter, exit, and move through the slide. In addition, you can use the Emphasis menu to make an element grow, shrink, or spin, or, if it is a text box, to make its font style or size change over time.

FEATURING INTERACTIVITY IN YOUR SLIDE SHOW: A NOTE ABOUT PERSONAL RESPONSE SYSTEMS

PowerPoint can be used to create slides that build interaction with your audience. You can show a photo or play an audio or a video clip and then ask the

REAL SPEAKERS IN ACTION

A Group Presentation

A group conducting a color forecast project for the automobile industry analyzed the history of automobile paint color choices and current market trends and then projected automobile paint colors for the 2010 model year. One group used i-clicker remotes to involve the audience during its presentation. When discussing current market trends, it queried audience members about the color of their personal vehicle. It also asked them what color new car or truck they would likely buy. Then, after the group presented its predictions for new automobile paint colors, it asked audience members which new color they would most likely buy. The audience enjoyed getting to play along with the presentation, and the group members focused on the audience and adjusted their comments accordingly. Can you think of other topics that would lend themselves to surveying your audience on the spot?

audience questions about it. If your speaking site is equipped with personal response system (PRS) technology, such as i-clicker, then you can survey your audience on the spot.

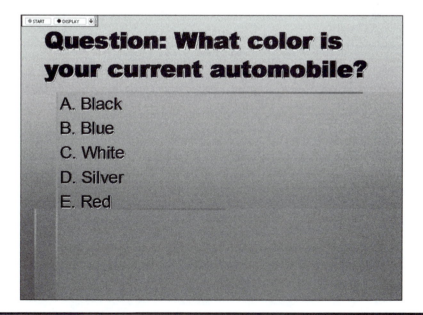

This is an example of a slide used to conduct an on-the-spot audience survey.

Using a PRS is especially helpful when you want to find out audience information that may be personal or embarrassing. A dentist giving a speech on brushing and flossing surveyed his audience in advance to find out how many times a day audience members brushed their teeth. That same survey could have been done in the middle of the presentation, but audience members would have been less likely to publicly admit that they did not brush their teeth that morning. A PRS gives audience members the comfort of anonymously answering questions. Even without a PRS at your disposal, involving audience members can increase their interest in your speech topic and improve their retention of the information you are trying to convey.

Preparation and Delivery: 4
Effectively Using Your Presentation Aid

ENSURING EFFECTIVE DELIVERY

So far we have discussed the ways in which you can use presentation software to help you capture and maintain audience attention, support your speech message and purpose, clarify complex information, and provide flexible, visual frameworks for presentations. And we have shown how, by following a few basic visual principles, it is possible to make a great slide show that closely follows your speech outline. However, for all of the prospective benefits of presentation software, there are also risks associated with delivering a speech with a slide show. The list of pros and cons in Chapter 1 introduced the possible risks of distracting the audience from the purpose of the speech, interfering with the smoothness of the presentation, and experiencing unexpected technical glitches. You have probably sat through many presentations, speeches, and lectures where speakers or instructors read verbatim from their wordy slides in boring, monotone voices. Clifford Stoll, the author of the article that follows, feels strongly that PowerPoint is not a constructive tool for public speakers. While you read the excerpt and discussion questions, think about how Stoll's objections to PowerPoint could be allayed or avoided with proper preparation and delivery. As you read the discussion about preparation and delivery that follows, reflect on the ways in which careful planning, diligent practice, and engaged delivery can help you avoid "The Plague of PowerPoint."

THE PLAGUE OF POWERPOINT

Perhaps you've not yet seen a PowerPoint talk. You soon will.

Imagine a boring slide show. Now add lots of generic, irrelevant, and pyrotechnic graphics. What have you got? A boring slide show, complete with irrelevant whizbang graphics.

Ten years ago, these computer graphics shows seemed futuristic. Today, they're hackneyed. PowerPoint is the enemy of a good talk.

Presentation software goes under several names: PowerPoint, Persuasion, Presentation, or Freelance. Promoted as the up-and-coming way to reach an audience, it's used by technical speakers, sales folk, instructors, lawyers, and, naturally, politicians.

These programs let anyone make transparencies or displays, complete with clip art, fancy backgrounds, and colorful charts. Used with a video projector, your audience can watch text scroll onto the screen accompanied by animated sprites and dancing corporate logos.

Used to be you'd watch someone stand before an audience and stammer through a talk, cued by index cards and an occasional transparency. The audience scribbled notes and tried not to yawn.

All that's changed, thanks to the convergence of personal computers, video projectors, and laser printers. Today, the lecturer fiddles with a computer, focuses the projector, and adjusts his microphone. He pushes a few buttons and up pops a perfectly laid-out computer graphics display. New graphics appear on command, usually as bullet points perfectly lined up in columns. The audience has been given paper copies of the show in advance, so they read the notes and try not to yawn.

Almost nobody likes to stand up and talk to an audience. Techies, accustomed to dealing with computers rather than people, are especially shy. So naturally they latch onto anything which will insulate them from this experience. In public speaking, PowerPoint is the coward's choice.

Once, foibles, yarns, and a few jokes sympathetically linked speaker to audience. Now, everyone's either staring at the video screen or reading their handouts. The speaker becomes an incidental accessory behind the lectern.

Not that the speaker cares. He's too busy fiddling with buttons and watching the screen. With his back to the audience, an orator knows what the next slide will say, as does the audience. Should he forget a line or head off on a tangent, the program prompts him back to the prepared talk.

Result: a predictable, pre-programmed, pre-produced lecture, devoid of any human content. The audience might as well watch a videotape.

Sure, meetings are notoriously tedious. And anything that can jazz 'em up is welcome. But PowerPoint and its cousins seem destined to make meetings even more boring.

This assumes that the electronics go right. If the computer hangs up, the software crashes, or the video projector flakes out, the speaker's cooked. He'll likely fumble with the cables or call for a technician. All of which wastes 5 or 10 minutes and completely derails his talk. I've watched it happen.

Oh, I admire the technical capabilities of these programs. With the right hookup, you can link to a Web site or copy graphs from a spreadsheet. You can include sound effects, cartoons, and clip art. But 100 people have gathered to connect with a speaker, not to watch a light show.

What motivates an audience? Emotion. Passion. Fire. A sense of warmth, excitement, shared adventure. A PowerPoint-driven meeting delivers chilly, pre-programmed video graphics. You see graphs, numbers, and bullet charts. But dancing sprites and flashing logos can't inspire zeal, loyalty, outrage, or a clarion call to action.

The computer-generated graphics draw the crowd's attention. Rather than watching you, the audience gazes at the fonts and animation. They're already holding your handouts, so there's no reason to take notes or intently listen for your important points. Indeed, since everything's on the screen and in the handouts, there's not much reason to listen to what you say.

We remember the performance, not a font or logo. We want to identify with the speaker, but it's hard to overcome the sterility of the computer graphics. When was the last time you saw an inspiring multimedia show? When was the last meeting you said, "Hey, those glitzy graphics sure impressed me!"

I can imagine Abraham Lincoln at Gettysburg, sporting a video projector and PowerPoint. He'd show a graphic of 87 calendars flipping by, fading into an animation of Washington crossing the Delaware. Highlighted on his bullet chart would be the phrases "A new nation," "Conceived in liberty," and "All men are created equal."

If only PowerPoint were confined to computer conferences, where it would just put techies to sleep. Alas, it's now showing up in schools. I sat through an American history class dulled by PowerPoint. The high school students sat glassy-eyed as their teacher read the text rolling up the screen. "Warren Harding was the 29th President and was born in Marion, Ohio. The five most important features of his administration were . . ." Deadly.

Kids latch onto this new way to slack off. A high school student from Wilsonville, Oregon, wrote this ungrammatical analysis: "I wasn't doing crap for a presentation that I had to do in class. But I still received a good grade, because it was on a PowerPoint stack that took me a half hour to make. There was others in the class that worked their butts off to memorize their presentation, and here am I up there just reading off my presentation that was being projected on the screen."

So it looks as if PowerPoint is fast becoming the replacement for the educational slide show. Just about as relevant, just about as interesting.

Want to make a splash at your next public talk? Know your material so well that you can speak off the cuff, without computer, laser pointer, or video projector. Scribble your important points on a chalkboard, and emphasize them with your voice. Face your audience, not that computer monitor.

Throw out that tired clip art and the clichés about the explosion of technology, the challenge of the future, and the crisis in education. Let me hear your voice, not a pre-programmed sound effect. Show me your ideas, not someone else's template.

Amaze me with your stories. Thrill me with your experiences. Astound me with your brilliance. Convince me with your passion. Show excitement. Intrigue. Anything—just don't bore me with another computer graphics presentation.

Source: Clifford Stoll. *High Tech Heretic: Why Computers Don't Belong in the Classroom and Other Reflections by a Computer Contrarian* (New York: Doubleday, 1999).

DISCUSSION QUESTIONS

1. What type of delivery does the author of this article wish to see from speakers?

2. What major complaints are voiced by the author regarding a speaker's use of PowerPoint slide shows? On what points do you agree with the author? On what points do you disagree? Why? How might you work to avoid some of the drawbacks the author describes?

3. The author makes a reference to historically famous speakers, such as Abraham Lincoln, and how a famous speech, such as the Gettysburg Address, would have been seriously flawed if PowerPoint technology had been available. When you think of other famous speakers, such as Martin Luther King Jr. or Ronald Reagan, do you imagine their speeches would have been different if they had used PowerPoint? Would the speeches have been better or worse? Why?

PLANNING FOR THE UNEXPECTED

Do not assume that the projection of your presentation aid will always go smoothly. Technology is a great thing—when it works! You will often develop slides on one computer but use a different computer for your presentation. Not all computers and user features of projection equipment are the same. You

CHECKLIST

Preparing Ahead to Avoid Common Technical Glitches

1. Check in advance that the operating system on the computer you will be using for your presentation is compatible with the operating system with which you created your aids.

2. Make sure that the version of the presentation software you utilized to develop your slide show (e.g., PowerPoint 2007) is identical to the version loaded onto the computer you will use for your presentation.

3. Save all of the files connected to your presentation in the same folder and onto the same disk.

4. Confirm that the computer you will be using will accept the Flash drive, zip drive, CD-ROM disk, or floppy disk on which you saved your presentation.

5. Make every effort to practice with the actual equipment you will be using to familiarize yourself with the organization and idiosyncrasies of the computer from which you will be projecting your presentation.

REAL SPEAKERS IN ACTION

The Importance of Thinking Ahead

Jameela, a student in a basic speech communication course, started putting together her visual aids three hours prior to giving her speech. She had a brief PowerPoint presentation that included diagrams that were crucial to explaining her topic, as well as a poster depicting a graph that she planned to use to help her audience visualize a specific statistic. When it was time to give her speech, she had trouble advancing the slides smoothly and struggled with the projector's remote control. Then the projector's bulb burned out, leaving her to depend on her other presentation aids. Unfortunately, once she was in front of the class, Jameela realized that although her poster was helpful it did not contain the most important diagrams needed to illustrate her topic. She tried to describe the diagrams as best she could, but since she had not prepared this explanation beforehand, it left her audience confused about the more technical aspects of her presentation.

With a contingency plan, Jameela may have been better prepared to deliver her speech and navigate technical challenges. She could have focused on the following suggestions to more effectively deploy her presentation aids:

1. Think carefully about how many presentation aids to include and when to use them.

2. Leave enough time to practice using your presentation aids with the actual equipment you will depend upon during the presentation.

3. Visualize ways to deal with possible technical glitches, including developing backup measures that you can substitute for your original presentation aids.

4. Talk with whomever is responsible for the speaking site, such as the speech instructor or office manager, early on in the speech preparation process so she or he will know what equipment you plan to use.

never know when a system may crash or when you may forget a log-in password. Sometimes your software may not be compatible with the software in the presentation room. Before you give your presentation, there are some specific steps you can take to ensure technical compatibility between your speech site and your slide show. The checklist on page 50 can help you steer clear of possible problems.

Even careful preparation cannot prevent every possible glitch. The best way to keep a technical glitch from becoming a disaster and ruining your speech is to devise a contingency plan. See the story above for an example of the value of a contingency plan. To create a plan, you will need to think about possible problems that may arise and develop solutions to those problems. Reflect on your expectations for the presentation before you begin to work on your presentation aids. Successful speakers often prepare two or more types of presentation aids (such as an object or a slide printout to accompany a PowerPoint presentation). If your slides cannot be used, will you still be able to deliver the speech? As backup measures, you may want to print out hard copies of your PowerPoint slides using the Handout Master, make overhead projector transparencies, or be prepared to draw a diagram on the board, if one is available. Anita, a pharmaceutical sales representative who lost her computer equipment and presentation aids on the way to a convention, still managed to give an informative, convincing sales pitch using a black marker and a large note pad. She was calm and confident because she had developed a contingency plan.

FAMILIARIZING YOURSELF WITH THE SPEAKING SITE AND EQUIPMENT

As your speech date draws near, it is crucial to consider the speaking site itself. If at all possible, visit the site to get a feel for what it is like, especially when you are going to be using technology in your presentation. If you are speaking at a site that is familiar to you, such as your usual conference room or classroom, you may think, "I'm in this room several times a week—I know what this site is like," but there is a big difference between sitting in a chair participating in a meeting or listening to a lecture and being the person in command of the equipment and the audience's attention. Visit your site again while visualizing yourself as the speaker. The best speakers schedule appointments prior to their speeches to scout out their speaking sites, to perform run-throughs, and to test the presentation aid equipment. If you are a student in a public speaking course, visiting the speech classroom outside of class can also present a great opportunity to go over any questions with your instructor and to get some speaking tips directly related to your speech assignment

Research has shown that speakers who are familiar with the surroundings in which the speech will occur may be less apprehensive. Walk around the room and visualize how close the audience will be, locate the light switch, and note how far the projection equipment is from the podium or speaking area. Is it possible to rearrange the furniture or equipment if it does not suit your needs? Is the podium adjustable to your height? How large is the room? Ask if you can visit the room on the day of your presentation to check the equipment and test your presentation aids.

Another concern when using presentation software is poor lighting and how to remedy it. You may have to shut off or dim the lights so your audience can view your slides. Turning the lights off while speaking may be a comforting thought for some apprehensive speakers, but it is not a good idea to have your audience sit in the dark. For one thing, this could encourage tired audience members to take a nap! In addition, speaking in a darkened room makes it difficult to maintain eye contact and to interact with your audience. Fortunately, newer projectors function well with the lights on, although the speaking site for your presentation may not have one of the latest projectors. For this reason, be sure to consider lighting conditions in your site analysis.

ACTIVITY

Designing Your Own Presentation Space

In this diagram of a typical classroom, you see twenty-four student desks, a computer desk, a podium, and the screen. Maybe the furniture could be arranged to better suit your topic or your presentation. Use the box below to draw your own ideal diagram for your speaking site. Indicate placement of furniture, such as seating for your audience, a podium for speaking, and any easels or display tables you will use in the space.

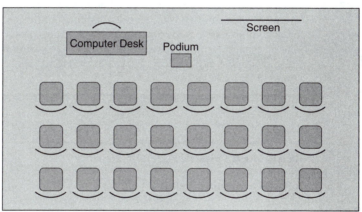

REAL SPEAKERS IN ACTION

A Negative Scouting Report

Several student speakers from three different colleges were giving a presentation at an undergraduate honors conference in Louisville, Kentucky. About six months prior to the conference, the students were told they would be in a large conference room with several round tables. Each college's group of student speakers thought it would be making its discussion-format presentation to a round table of students and faculty advisors on a rotating basis. Each group was supposed to take fifteen minutes at each round table: five minutes for presenting its information and ten minutes for discussing the topic with participants at the table.

However, the students did not scout out the site, and when they arrived, they were in a smaller room than they expected, with rows of chairs for the attendees instead of round tables. Additionally, student speakers had no place to put their posters and handouts. Overall, the conference attendees were satisfied with the presentations, but the student speakers felt uncomfortable, lacked cohesion, and looked unprofessional as they juggled their presentation aids. If the speakers had scouted out the site earlier in the day, they could have adapted to the speech site and arranged for a display table.

REAL SPEAKERS IN ACTION

A Positive Scouting Report

Chen was asked to give a presentation at a conference in St. Paul. He knew that he would be speaking to about 100 people in a hotel conference room equipped with projection equipment. Based on this information, Chen began to draft his remarks and prepare his slides. One of the first things he did when he arrived at the hotel was visit the room where he would be making his presentation. This visit was pivotal to the success of his speech. Chen got a sense of the place and eased his worries that the room was going to be too small or too big or would not have the computer hardware or software to support his speech. He spent about ten minutes thinking about the space and how he could best reach his audience. Apparently, it was time well spent, because he received the highest audience ranking of all the speakers at the conference.

USING EQUIPMENT EFFECTIVELY

You may find useful the following PowerPoint presentation developed for students in an introductory speech class, both for the information on how to use presentation aid equipment and as an example of a PowerPoint slide show. For additional information about the specific equipment in your presentation room, ask the coordinator of the space, such as the office manager, audiovisual or technological specialist, or instructor of your class, who may have access to the manuals that accompany the projection equipment and/or much practical experience operating the projection system.

Using Classroom Equipment for your Presentation

By:
Assistant Professor Brian Kline &
Assistant Professor Allison Ainsworth
Area of Communication Studies

Turning the computer on...

- If the LED (blue) light is not glowing on the computer front, then the computer is off.
- Push the power button.

Loading your visual aid

1. Log in to the computer with your id and password.
2. Insert your CD, floppy disk, or flash drive in the appropriate slot.
3. Open your document.

TIP: You can also open your document as an attachment from your email account or from the shared network files.

Turning the projector on...

- If the projector lamp is not glowing, then the projector is off.
- Push the power button once.

It's on, but I don't see anything!

- The computer is on.
- Your power point slide is visible on the computer screen, but not on the large screen.
- The projector lamp is glowing.
- Push the blank button to open the shutter.

Showing a video clip

- Turn the DVD/VCR player on, and insert your disk or tape.
- Push the video button on the projector remote.

TIP: You can leave your power point open while showing the video clip.

Displaying the computer screen again.

- Be sure that the computer screen has the document you want displayed.
- Push the computer button on the projector remote.

Changing Power Point Slides

- This is a wireless mouse or remote control mouse.
- It is used to change your slides, to move the cursor, to open menu boxes, or to highlight items on your slide.

Changing Power Point Slides

- Advance to the next slide by pushing the left click button.

Changing Power Point Slides

- Oops! A menu popped up onto the screen. You pushed the right click button by mistake.
- Move the cursor arrow by using this toggle.
- Select previous by pushing the left click button.

Changing Power Point Slides

- To use the laser pointer to highlight an item on your slide.
- Push the little round button.
- While keeping button pressed, aim at screen.

Ending slide show

- Push the right click to view menu selection.
- Select End Show.
- Close your document.
- Blank the screen using the projector remote; push the blank button.

Turning the projector off...

- Save the expensive light bulb by turning off the projector when not in use.
- Push the power button on the projector remote twice.

Logging off the computer...

- Be courteous! Log off the computer, so that the next user doesn't have to log you off before logging in.
- Leave the computer on unless directed to turn off by instructor. Shut down the computer before pushing the power button.

PRACTICE, PRACTICE, PRACTICE

If at all possible, make an appointment with a coworker, your instructor, or a speech tutor for a practice session in your presentation room, with the equipment you will be using the day of your speech. The importance of practicing your speech with your presentation aid cannot be overemphasized. This will give you the experience and confidence to deliver your speech and utilize your aid effectively and will help reduce speech anxiety. If there is a time limit for your presentation, then practicing your speech with a stopwatch or clock is a must. Rehearse your speech until you have stayed within the time limit at least three times. If you are having trouble doing so, then you may need to change your speech or presentation aid and then schedule another practice session to confirm that you are adhering to the time limit. You may also want to practice your speech in front of different audiences: some coworkers, your speech tutor, other students, or your instructor. Ask each of them for constructive criticism so you can improve your speech. Practice is the key to making a successful presentation.

DELIVERY WITH A PRESENTATION AID

A smooth delivery will integrate your presentation aids into your speech and will display them so the audience can reap maximum benefit with minimum distraction or confusion. Remember, never read directly from the slides, although you can glance at them just long enough to confirm that the correct ones are being projected. The slides are for the audience. You should be able to deliver an interesting speech even without presentation aids.

Note that fluency, discussed in Chapter 3, is also affected by factors of delivery: how smoothly you progress through your slides. You need to develop your slide show content and design for fluency, but you also need to click the remote control at just the right moment so the next slide coordinates with the words you are speaking. Be sure to allow enough time for the audience to absorb the content of your slide before you move on to the next one. Even if you have an organized, well-written speech, an effective vocal delivery, and a well-designed slide show, your presentation can still lack fluency if your slide show is poorly integrated into your speech. The tips that follow can assist you in a strong speech delivery.

CHECKLIST

Delivery Tips

1. Make eye contact with your audience. Do not read from the slide.

2. Practice changing slides until you can do it seamlessly.

3. If you are not comfortable with technology, then practice ahead of time with someone who is.

4. Do not interrupt the flow of your speech to ask for help with the equipment. Stay focused on the topic; if you have technical problems, initiate your backup plan.

5. Use the blank or AV Mute function to hide your presentation aid until you are ready.

6. Avoid talking while preparing your slide show; remain silent until you are ready to begin your speech.

7. Be flexible. It is acceptable to make changes during your presentation, or to skip a slide or return to a slide to emphasize a point. You are running the presentation aid—it is not running you.

8. If you use automatic slide change features, then be sure to rehearse delivering your speech with the actual equipment you will be using, since that equipment may not operate at the same speed as your home computer.

9. Remember that using too many images, too much text, or too many media clips can bore or overwhelm an audience.

PREPARING AND DELIVERING AN ONLINE SPEECH

Some virtual presentations use Web cams and conference-hosting Web sites that enable participants to log in at the same time to either make or view a presentation. Other online presentations involve people uploading video clips of their speeches being delivered to live audiences at physical locations. And sometimes people develop PowerPoint slide shows that represent the speech without an actual delivery.

If you are not making an in-person presentation, then you may need to provide more detail or text on your slides, verify that your Web hyperlinks are active, and remove any animation features so the reader can progress through the slide show at a comfortable pace. To "practice" your speech for this online context, simply ask other people to read through your PowerPoint slide show without interruption. Then use their constructive criticism to make any needed changes. Reading aloud your online PowerPoint presentation can also help you make any necessary corrections. The delivery tips for speeches made in front of Web cams or video cameras are the same as for live presentations. Treat the camera lens as the audience, and make eye contact with it.

CONCLUSION

Your real challenge now is to adapt the material in this guide to your own unique speaking situation. You will certainly achieve excellent results if you follow the advice herein. Be sure to focus the majority of your energy on speech planning; tailor your presentation generally—and your aids specifically—to the needs of your audience; take into account the speech forum; adhere to basic design principles; create a contingency plan in case your initial approach to incorporating aids does not work out; and, by all means, practice, practice, practice.

When armed with a carefully prepared presentation and aids that support your speech goals, you will be able to make complex ideas clear, to capture and hold your audience's interest, and to help your audience recall your message. You should feel confident that the ability to give a great speech accompanied by effective presentation software will prove to be a powerful skill that serves you well in the future. Good luck!